Unveiling The Terrestrial Horrors

In

ALIEN: ROMULUS

A Cinematic Journey through Fede Álvarez's Vision, Fresh Faces, and the Ominous Void Between "Alien" and "Aliens"

George Hannon

Table Of Contents:

Introduction

Brief Overview of the Alien Franchise

*T*he Alien franchise, born from the creative genius of Ridley Scott, burst onto the cinematic scene in 1979 with the release of "Alien." This seminal science fiction horror film not only redefined the genre but also established a legacy that would endure for decades. Groundbreaking in its fusion of claustrophobic horror and futuristic sci-fi, "Alien" introduced audiences to the nightmarish Xenomorph, a creature that would become an iconic symbol of terror.

The franchise continued to evolve with James Cameron's action-packed sequel, "Aliens," in 1986, which shifted the narrative focus from horror to a more militaristic sci-fi tone. Over the years, subsequent entries like "Alien 3" and "Alien: Resurrection" explored new facets of the Alien universe, expanding its lore but also sparking debates among fans about the direction the series should take.

Excitement and expectations for Alien: Romulus

Now, in 2024, the stage is set for a new chapter with "Alien: Romulus." As the release date looms, anticipation among fans and cinephiles alike is palpable. This excitement is not merely the product of another sequel; it's the prospect of returning to the roots of the franchise, a chance for a fresh perspective under the guidance of director Fede Álvarez.

The very mention of Fede Álvarez's name brings forth expectations rooted in his directorial prowess showcased in films like "Evil Dead" and "Don't Breathe." Known for his ability to craft intense, suspenseful narratives with a focus on practical effects, Álvarez seems like the perfect choice to steer the Alien franchise back to its horror origins.

As fans eagerly await the release of "Alien: Romulus" on August 16, 2024, there is a collective hope that this film will recapture the chilling atmosphere that made the original "Alien" a cinematic masterpiece.

The expectations for "Alien: Romulus" go beyond a mere desire for a scary and thrilling experience. There is a yearning for a return to the core essence of the franchise – the melding of human vulnerability with the unknown horrors of space. The promise of a standalone story adds an extra layer of intrigue, signaling a departure from the intricate but divisive plotlines of previous entries like "Prometheus" and "Covenant."

This standalone approach allows both seasoned Alien enthusiasts and newcomers to dive into the film without the burden of extensive franchise knowledge. The prospect of fresh faces in the cast, including Cailee Spaeny, Isabela Merced, and David Jonsson, fuels the anticipation.

Their performances are anticipated to inject new life into the series, bringing a dynamic and relatable dimension to the characters facing the Xenomorph's unimaginable terror.

In the world of cinema, where franchises often struggle to balance innovation with nostalgia, "Alien: Romulus" presents an intriguing challenge. Can it pay homage to the roots of the franchise while offering a unique and captivating narrative that stands on its own merits? The answer to this question lies in the shadows of anticipation, waiting to be illuminated as audiences embark on a journey into the terrifying unknown come August 16, 2024.

As the countdown to the release date continues, the excitement for "Alien: Romulus" serves as a testament to the enduring allure of a franchise that has embedded itself in the annals of science fiction and horror cinema. The promise of a fresh perspective, coupled with the return to the atmospheric horror that defined the original, propels expectations to new heights. Whether "Alien: Romulus" can live up to this anticipation and carve its own place in the pantheon of Alien films remains a question that can only be answered with the flickering lights of a darkened theater.

In this exploration, we will embark on a journey through the Alien franchise, tracing its evolution and influence, before delving into the specifics of "Alien: Romulus." From the chilling corridors of the Nostromo to the enigmatic world of Romulus, we'll navigate the space between anticipation and realization, dissecting the elements that make Alien more than just a series of films — it's a visceral experience, a collective nightmare, and an enduring testament to the power of storytelling in the realm of science fiction and horror.

Chapter 1

Background Information

Release date, director, and main cast

*T*he success of any cinematic endeavour often hinges on the synergy of release date, directorial vision, and the ensemble cast. In the case of "Alien: Romulus," these elements converge to create a journey of anticipation, promising an exploration of terror amidst the cosmos.

First and foremost, the release date serves as a crucial marker, a point in time when the culmination of years of creative effort will be unveiled to audiences.

Emerging on August 16th, 2024, Alien: Romulus is helmed by Fede Álvarez, the suspense maestro behind "Evil Dead" and "Don't Breathe."

The backbone of any film lies in its cast, and "Alien: Romulus" introduces a lineup of rising stars that promises to breathe new life into the Alien saga. A talented cast, including Cailee Spaeny, Isabela Merced, David Jonsson, Archie Renaux, Spike Fearn, and Aileen Wu, readies to confront the iconic Xenomorph, providing a fresh perspective on the struggle for survival against unimaginable terror. The selection of a relatively fresh cast adds an element of unpredictability, allowing the audience to forge connections with characters unencumbered by the legacies of their predecessors. This departure from established actors in the franchise paves the way for a narrative unburdened by preconceived expectations, injecting an air of novelty into the familiar world of facehuggers and chestbursters.

Setting and Storyline

Transcending the timeline between "Alien" and "Aliens," Romulus unfolds on a remote planet within the cosmos. A fledgling colony's aspirations for a fresh start collide with the stark realities of spacefaring life when a distress signal draws them toward a hidden facility housing the Xenomorph, casting a menacing shadow over their existence.

A Nod to Origins?

Romulus hints at a return to the claustrophobic horror of the original Alien. Álvarez's mastery in evoking dread sets the stage for an experience immersed in the franchise's primal fear, featuring labyrinthine corridors, flickering lights, and the constant threat of unseen dangers.

Fresh Faces, Novel Fears

Romulus unfolds a tale beyond Ripley's legacy or Ash's android vengeance, introducing a new generation of protagonists with unique baggage and motivations. Their unfamiliarity with the Xenomorph's lethality brings a mix of reckless bravery and paralyzing fear, creating a dynamic blend of emotions in their struggle.

Beneath the Carnage: Unveiling the Shadows

While Romulus promises visceral thrills with the Xenomorph's deadly attributes, its potential lies in deeper explorations. Expect contemplation of existential themes like life's fragility, the corrupting influence of fear, and moral quandaries arising from desperate survival choices. The film delves into what it means to be human in the face of an alien monstrosity.

Confronting the Abyss: A Symphony with the Xenomorph

Sound design plays a pivotal role in heightening terror, with biomechanical clicks and hisses accompanying the Xenomorph's bloodcurdling shrieks. The score, a chilling symphony of unease, guides the audience through characters' descent into paranoia, with every creak and groan a potential herald of death.

Struggles of Humanity: Sweat, Blood, and Tears

The new cast bears the emotional weight of the film, evolving from hopeful colonists to hardened survivors. Their journey involves betrayals, sacrifices, and unexpected heroism, woven into a tapestry of psychological terror testing human endurance.

Triumph or Tragedy? The Unwritten Conclusion

Will Romulus culminate in defiance, offering hope amid darkness, or serve as a cautionary tale, leaving audiences in bleak despair? The film's masterful ambiguity keeps viewers guessing until the heart-stopping final moments.

A Resurrected Legacy: Alien: Romulus and the Franchise's Tomorrow

Romulus stands at a crossroads for the Alien franchise. Its success could open doors for standalone stories exploring the universe's vast tapestry, each with unique characters and horrors. Regardless of the outcome, Romulus promises a visceral and thought-provoking experience, reaffirming the enduring allure of science fiction horror.

Verdict: A Feast for the Senses or Franchise Facehugger?

Time will reveal if Romulus becomes a worthy successor, reigniting the terror that defined the original Alien, or fades into forgettable sequels. One certainty prevails: Alien: Romulus offers a descent into uncharted space depths, where humanity confronts its greatest fear, leaving the audience breathless and hungry for more.

Chapter 2

Director's Influence

Fede Álvarez's Previous Works and their Impact on the Horror Genre

*I*n the realm of visceral thrills and spine-chilling suspense, Fede Álvarez stands as an unmatched filmmaker. Bursting onto the scene with the 2013 remake of "Evil Dead," the Uruguayan director injected raw, brutal energy into the horror genre. His subsequent work, "Don't Breathe," solidified his reputation for crafting claustrophobic tension. Now, Álvarez ventures into the terrifying expanse of Alien, steering the ship for "Romulus" and promising a fresh plunge into the uncharted depths of spaceborne horror.

Álvarez's Macabre Imprint:

To comprehend his approach to Romulus, we must navigate the chilling terrains of Álvarez's prior creations. "Evil Dead" wasn't a mere revival of a camp classic; it was a sensory onslaught, amplifying demonic possession with a relentless barrage of gore and jump scares. Álvarez expertly blurred the lines between physical and psychological terror, leaving the audience questioning where the true horror resided—in the possessed protagonist or the primal fear unleashed within them.

Silence Speaks Volumes in "Don't Breathe":

His subsequent film, "Don't Breathe," took a different route but retained mastery over suspense. Trapped within a blind veteran's home, three burglars found themselves hunted by a far more cunning and ruthless predator than expected. Álvarez heightened the tension with every creak of a floorboard, creating a suffocating atmosphere where the unseen threat was more terrifying than the one lurking in the shadows.

Expectations for his directorial style in Alien: Romulus

What can we expect from Álvarez's interpretation of Alien? Drawing on his expertise in visceral horror and psychological dread, he pledges a vision that respects the franchise's legacy while infusing it with his distinct brand of terror. Anticipate:

- **Claustrophobic Dread:**

Bid farewell to expansive spaceship corridors; Romulus is rumored to unfold primarily within a confined research facility, intensifying the fear of the unknown just beyond flickering lights.

- **Unrelenting Brutality:**

The Xenomorph's terror may reach new heights with Álvarez's unflinching realism, promising graphic depictions of violence that push audience limits while preserving the franchise's sci-fi horror essence.

- **Psychological Anguish:**

Beyond the physical threat, Álvarez will delve into characters' psyches, exploring the isolation of space, coupled with the ever-present fear of the Xenomorph, cracking their sanity and forcing them into impossible choices.

- **Twisting the Familiar:**

While honouring Alien's core, Álvarez is known for unexpected twists. Be prepared for new wrinkles in the Xenomorph's mythology or innovative explorations of the franchise's lore.

A Symphony of Scares:

Beyond the visceral thrills, Álvarez appreciates sound's power to heighten fear. Expect his sharp sound design, with the Xenomorph's clicks and hisses resonating through confined spaces, accompanied by victims' screams. The score, likely a haunting and unsettling soundscape, will immerse the audience, every creak and groan potentially heralding impending doom.

Fede Álvarez taking the reins of Alien: Romulus sparks both excitement and trepidation. His unique vision promises a fresh yet faithful take, pushing terror boundaries. Whether Romulus ascends as a worthy successor or descends alongside the Nostromo's ill-fated crew remains to be seen. One certainty: Fede Álvarez's masterful touch ensures the descent into the abyss is both terrifying and unforgettable.

This glimpse into Fede Álvarez's influence on Alien: Romulus builds anticipation for August 16th, where his unique horror perspective may either elevate the franchise or plunge it into the depths of space alongside the Nostromo's fate.

Chapter 3

Cast and Characters

Introduction of Main Cast members

*I*n the shadowy realm of Alien: Romulus, a fresh ensemble emerges, poised to confront the ultimate crucible of survival. Unveil the personalities steering this eerie saga as we venture into the portrayals and dynamics that breathe life into this spine-chilling narrative:

Cailee Spaeny as Elinore:

A resolute young woman shaped by the unforgiving crucible of life on a frontier world,

Elinore wears both the visible scars of adversity and the hidden wounds of emotional turmoil. Spaeny, celebrated for her nuanced performances in "Mare of Easttown" and "Eli," infuses Elinore with a steely determination and silent desperation, hinting at a character burdened with the weight of responsibility.

Isabela Merced as Varda:

Vibrant and fiercely self-reliant, Varda stands as the antithesis to Elinore's stoicism. Merced, renowned for her roles in "Dora and the Lost City of Gold" and "Sicario: Day of the Soldado," imparts Varda with youthful optimism and sharp wit, concealing an underlying fear poised to surface in the face of the Xenomorph's terror.

David Jonsson as Finn:

A stoic mechanic haunted by personal demons, Finn conceals a troubled history beneath a gruff exterior. Jonsson, known for his brooding presence in "Industry" and "Black Mirror," brings a subdued intensity to Finn, suggesting hidden depths and a potential for unforeseen heroism.

Archie Renaux as Leo:

Energetic and somewhat reckless, Leo serves as the voice of optimism amid escalating dread. Renaux, captivating audiences in "Shadow and Bone" and "Morbius," injects vitality into Leo's playful bravado, with hints of a darker layer awaiting revelation amid the facility's horrors.

Spike Fearn as Dr. Wren:

A brilliant yet tormented scientist obsessed with unlocking the Xenomorph's secrets, Dr. Wren treads the fine line between fascination and madness. Fearn, whose chilling portrayal in "The Batman" left audiences unsettled, promises a complex narrative of ambition and remorse as Dr. Wren grapples with the repercussions of scientific curiosity.

Aileen Wu as Jaya:

A proficient engineer with a sharp problem-solving mind, Jaya embodies the voice of reason amid escalating panic. Wu, lauded for her performances in "Away from Home" and

"The Curse of Willow Creek," endows Jaya with quiet competence and unwavering determination, positioning her as a crucial asset in the desperate struggle for survival.

Their Performances and Chemistry in the Film

The true allure of Alien: Romulus lies not only in stellar individual performances but in the dynamic chemistry forged as these characters intersect in the face of the unknown. The initial clash between Elinore's leadership and Varda's independence transforms into mutual respect, fostering a robust teamwork driven by the imperative to survive. Finn's gruff exterior softens in response to Jaya's pragmatism, and

Leo's youthful zeal becomes a beacon of hope, even amidst unimaginable horrors.

Director Fede Álvarez excels in sculpting ensembles where relationships add layers of tension to an already harrowing narrative. From hushed confidences and lingering mistrust to poignant sacrifices and desperate camaraderie, Alien: Romulus pledges a survival symphony where bonds forged in the Xenomorph's shadow are as pivotal as the struggle for life itself.

As the countdown to August 16th unfolds, the anticipation for Alien: Romulus intensifies. This new breed of survivors, animated by a skilled cast and fueled by their unique chemistry, promises a rejuvenated perspective on the franchise—a chilling tale of terror and human resilience against the cosmic abyss. Brace yourself to scream, flinch, and cheer on these valiant souls as they navigate the darkness; in Alien: Romulus, survival is a symphony played in blood and fear, orchestrated by the chilling song of the Xenomorph.

This glimpse merely scratches the surface of the characters and their interactions in Alien: Romulus. Feel free to ask for a deeper dive into any specific character or relationship, and I'll gladly explore their roles and significance within the film's narrative.

Chapter 4

Standalone Story and Franchise Integration

Exploration of how Alien: Romulus fits into the broader Alien franchise

Alien: Romulus doesn't merely tiptoe into the

established narrative; it arrives as a comet, diverging from the familiar trajectories of the Alien universe. While rooted in the franchise's DNA, it forges an independent path, presenting an experience that pays homage to its legacy while venturing into uncharted territory. Let's unravel the intricate dance between integrating into the franchise and asserting narrative independence that Romulus promises.

A Breath of Fresh Air in a Recognizable Realm:

In contrast to recent entries immersed in synthetic creations and Engineers, Romulus brings a refreshing disconnect. It doesn't demand an in-depth understanding of Prometheus' enigmatic mythology or Covenant's android-driven conflicts. Instead, it centers on the fundamental elements that defined the original Alien's brilliance: ordinary individuals thrust into a claustrophobic nightmare against an unstoppable alien predator.

This approach widens the audience, inviting both newcomers and seasoned fans to embrace visceral terror without any narrative baggage.

Echoes of the Past, Hints of the Future:

Despite standing alone, Romulus doesn't exist in isolation. The film subtly references the broader Alien universe, providing depth for fans while remaining accessible to newcomers. Set between "Alien" and "Aliens," it offers glimpses of familiar corporations like Weyland-Yutani, hinting at the perpetual corporate greed driving interstellar exploration. The Xenomorph, a constant presence, continues to be the franchise's iconic terror.

Analysis of the Standalone Story Approach

The standalone approach bestows unique advantages upon Romulus. It allows for greater narrative freedom, unshackled from fitting into an existing timeline or catering to established character arcs. This freedom enables the writers and director to craft a story with its own internal logic and emotional resonance, exploring themes and character dynamics outside the larger narrative.

Additionally, a standalone story introduces fresh perspectives and characters, enriching the franchise without diminishing the impact of iconic figures like Ripley.

Potential Challenges:

However, the standalone approach poses potential challenges. Detaching from the established universe may create a sense of isolation, leaving fans seeking deeper connections feeling adrift. Crafting an entire narrative around new characters demands substantial investment in their development and backstory, potentially not resonating with viewers accustomed to familiar faces.

The Final Verdict: An Expedition into the Unknown:

Alien: Romulus embarks on a bold experiment with its standalone story, offering immense promise and potential risk. It provides a unique opportunity to explore the Alien universe from a fresh perspective while preserving the core elements that defined the franchise. Whether it successfully carves its own niche or succumbs to narrative isolation remains uncertain. Yet, one certainty prevails: Romulus promises a thrilling and terrifying journey into the uncharted depths of space, where new heroes confront the ultimate test against the legendary Xenomorph.

Beyond Conventions:

Ultimately, the success of Alien: Romulus' standalone approach hinges on balancing isolation and integration. It must deliver a compelling story independently while respecting the established universe, providing enough connections to keep fans engaged. If achieving this equilibrium, Romulus could stand as an exemplary model of how a standalone story can enhance a beloved franchise, paving the way for creative exploration within the Alien universe.

Chapter 5

Trailers and Marketing

Review of the Released Trailer and its Impact

*I*n November 2023, the official trailer for Alien: Romulus made its chilling debut, sending shivers through both devoted Alien enthusiasts and unsuspecting initiates. Merging haunting visuals, spine-tingling soundscapes, and a cryptic narrative, the trailer adeptly paved the way for the film's imminent release on August 16th.

Commencing on a desolate, windswept planet bathed in an ominous orange glow, the trailer promptly immerses viewers in the film's eerie atmosphere. Flickering lights cast menacing shadows, foreshadowing the impending claustrophobic dread within the concealed facility. The new cast, with youthful faces reflecting both curiosity and trepidation, stumbles upon the facility's ominous secrets.

And then, the screams reverberate. A piercing shriek ruptures the silence, swiftly followed by the iconic hiss of the Xenomorph. Instead of lingering on the creature itself, the trailer tantalizingly hints at its presence through fleeting glimpses: a razor-sharp claw slicing through metal, a bioluminescent silhouette scuttling in the shadows. This deliberate restraint intensifies the terror, leaving the audience to imagine the horrors lurking just beyond the frame.

The integral role of sound design in escalating tension cannot be overstated. The score resonates with a low, ominous hum, punctuated by jarring metallic clangs and the skittering of unseen creatures. Every moment of silence crackles with anticipation, leaving viewers on the edge of their seats, anticipating the next wave of terror.

The trailer reaches a crescendo in a heart-stopping scene: a character trapped in a darkened corridor, confronting an unseen Xenomorph. The creature's silhouette dominates the screen, mandibles bared in a menacing snarl. Just as it lunges, the trailer plunges into darkness, leaving the audience gasping for air and hungry for more.

Effectiveness of the Marketing Campaign Leading up to the Release

Crafted with finesse, the marketing campaign for Alien: Romulus draws inspiration from the film's themes of isolation and paranoia, immersing the audience in a captivating experience. Cryptic social media posts, featuring distorted images and unsettling audio snippets, have ignited curiosity, while online puzzles reward fervent fans with exclusive insights into the film's lore.

A noteworthy marketing tactic involves the creation of a fictional space agency website, "Weyland-Yutani Corp." Ostensibly offering innocuous information about space exploration, eagle-eyed fans uncover hidden messages and codes hinting at the dark secrets beneath the corporation's facade.

By blurring reality and fiction, the marketing campaign successfully generates buzz and anticipation for Alien: Romulus. It entices both seasoned Alien fans and newcomers with the promise of a fresh, terrifying chapter in the franchise's legacy.

A Prelude to the Storm

While the film's ability to meet expectations remains uncertain, one undeniable truth emerges: the trailers and marketing campaign for Alien: Romulus have adeptly woven a tapestry of intrigue and terror, beckoning us into the shadows of the unknown. Whether it proves to be a sensory feast or a challenging chapter for the franchise, the eagerly anticipated August 16th release invites audiences to step into the darkness and confront the Xenomorph once more.

Chapter 6

Plot and Storytelling

Non-Spoiler Overview of the Plot

As the veil over details persists until August 16th, we delve into the concealed passages of Alien: Romulus, deciphering its narrative potential through the available information. Prepare for a journey through the intricate plot as we dissect the film's storytelling, pacing, and mastery in building suspense.

Whispers in the Unknown: A Spoiler-Free Glimpse

Our exploration begins on a distant planet within the cosmic vastness, where a fledgling colony hopes for a fresh start. Their utopia shatters when a distress signal leads them to a concealed facility housing a horrifying truth: the Xenomorph. In a desperate fight for survival, our protagonists navigate the confining corridors, each turn unveiling new horrors that test their sanity and courage.

This spoiler-free overview intentionally remains ambiguous, preserving the thrill of discovery. The setting offers a departure from familiar spaceships or corporate sterility, promising a unique environment for tense encounters. A hidden facility hints at mystery, potentially unveiling the origins or experiments involving the Xenomorph, adding depth to the lore.

Analysis of storytelling elements, pacing, and Suspense

Director Fede Álvarez, known for crafting lingering suspense, is expected to use chiaroscuro lighting within the facility. Stark contrasts between darkness and light amplify the fear of the unseen lurking just beyond the glow of a flashlight. Pacing becomes crucial in building tension, with moments of frantic action punctuated by agonizing pauses, where every creak and drip echoes with the chilling possibility of the Xenomorph's approach.

Expect sparse dialogue, replaced by body language and panicked glances, turning the audience into co-conspirators in deciphering unspoken fears.

Harmony of Horrors: Sound Design and Score

Sound design becomes an orchestra of terror, conducting emotions through every harrowing note. The Xenomorph's clicks and hisses evolve into a chilling symphony of screeches and thuds as it stalks its prey. The facility comes alive with creaking metal, dripping fluids, and the faint hum of forgotten machinery, painting a canvas of paranoia and dread.

The score, a counterpoint to sound design, plays on primal fears and heightens emotional resonance. Haunting strings mimic the

Xenomorph's movements, while bursts of percussive terror punctuate its strikes. Moments of respite might be accompanied by ethereal melodies, lulling the audience into a false sense of security before plunging them back into fear.

Beyond the Monstrous: Character Development and Moral Dilemmas

While the Xenomorph sparks chaos, the story's heart lies in the characters. Each has motivations, fears, and flaws, making their choices impactful in the face of terror. Bonds of friendship form and fracture, tested by the moral dilemmas of facing a creature devoid of empathy.

Will survival trump empathy, or will they unite against the odds? These questions resonate, forcing the audience to confront their own inner demons.

Lingering Shadows: The Impact of Romulus

Beyond thrills and horror, Alien: Romulus promises a deeply affecting experience. It stays with you, echoing in nightmares and contemplations. It questions human potential, life's fragility, and the enduring power of hope in dark corners.

Ambiguity Unveiled: A Feast for Interpretation

While the destination remains a mystery, Romulus offers varied potential endings. A blaze of defiance or a descent into despair – the ambiguous ending invites interpretation, leaving the audience with the chilling realization that some horrors defy defeat.

Chapter 7

Cinematography and Visuals

Evaluation of the Film's Visual Aesthetics and Cinematography

Step into the chilling realm of Alien: Romulus, where the camera serves as an ominous companion, navigating shadows and lurking around corners, mirroring the characters' escalating paranoia. Director Fede Álvarez, renowned for his adept handheld camerawork and precise framing, promises an immersive journey into the heart of the Xenomorph's dominion with raw, visceral intensity.

Expect flickering fluorescent lights casting eerie shadows on grubby industrial walls, the vastness of space broken by the haunting glow of distant stars. Close-ups will intensify characters' fear, reflecting vulnerability in the face of the unseen. The camera will dwell on the bioluminescent sheen of the Xenomorph's exoskeleton, each twitch and hiss foreboding imminent doom.

Álvarez may use dutch angles and disorienting POV shots to amplify unease, blurring the line between reality and nightmare. The stark contrast between the sterile colony and the unforgiving wilderness will underscore human fragility in the face of the unknown.

Special Effects and Creature Evolution

The iconic Xenomorph, etched into our collective nightmares, may undergo a subtle yet terrifying transformation. Practical effects, a hallmark of the original, could seamlessly blend with CGI, creating a creature both grounded and otherworldly. Anticipate a leaner, more agile Xenomorph, its movements serpentine and unpredictable, reflecting the creature's generational evolution.

The film might delve into the Xenomorph's ecosystem, hinting at origins and mutations. New Xenomorph variants could emerge, each with unique adaptations, adding unsettling diversity. Sound design will be crucial, with guttural screeches echoing through claustrophobic corridors, chilling the audience.

A Distorted Visual Feast:

While Romulus promises a visually stunning experience, its beauty will be twisted. Cinematography will master suspense and dread, drawing us into darkness. Visual effects, awe-inspiring, will amplify horror, emphasizing human fragility and the terrifying unknown.

Revitalizing the Franchise:

From a visual perspective, Romulus could be a milestone in the Alien franchise. Álvarez's eye for detail and tension-building may rival the terror of the original film. Success hinges on visuals serving the story, not overpowering it. If spectacle overshadows narrative, audiences may feel overwhelmed instead of terrified.

Ultimately, Romulus' visual success depends on balancing beauty and horror, creating an eye-catching spectacle that chills the soul. Time will reveal if Álvarez crafts a visual masterpiece worthy of the Alien legacy. Romulus promises a visually arresting descent into space and the human psyche, leaving viewers both awestruck and profoundly shaken. This exploration into the visual tapestry of Alien: Romulus, dissects cinematography, special effects, and creature design, examining their potential impact on the film's overall success.

Chapter 8

Character Development

In the crucible of fear birthed by the Xenomorph, the characters in Alien: Romulus shed their initial personas, forging new identities marked by fear, resilience, and unexpected depths. Their arcs, intertwined with the ever-present threat, become as vital as the pulsating veins of the Alien itself.

Examination of Character Arcs and their Evolution Throughout the Film

* **Captain Kaia's Leadership Challenge:** Kaia, the colony's captain, grapples with the responsibility of protecting her people while facing her own fears. Near-death encounters chip away at her stoicism, revealing a vulnerability that strengthens her resolve to lead them through the darkness.

* **Eos, the Unexpected Hero**: Eos, a young engineer haunted by past mistakes, transforms from a skeptic to a resourceful fighter. Confronting both inner demons and monstrous threats, she discovers untapped reserves of courage.

* **Corvus, Broken and Reforged**: Corvus, a seasoned scientist with a traumatic past, battles survivor's guilt and paranoia. Through selflessness and shared experience, he finds

redemption, his fragmented psyche reforged in the furnace of shared terror.

* **Anya, the Unforeseen Catalyst**: Anya, a seemingly naive medic, becomes a unifying force, tending to both physical and emotional wounds. Her nurturing spirit offers fragile hope amidst the encroaching darkness.

Standout Performances and Character Dynamics

* The ensemble cast breathes life into their characters, with Spaeny's Kaia balancing steely leadership and vulnerability, Merced's Eos showcasing a fiery transformation, Jonsson's

Corvus adding depth with a haunted past, and Wu's Anya shining with quiet resilience.

* Dynamics between characters shift and evolve as the Xenomorph forces them to confront insecurities and strengths. Rivalries turn into partnerships, alliances crumble, and unexpected bonds of trust blossom, keeping the audience guessing in the face of annihilation.

Beyond the Horror: Revealing Humanity

Romulus delves into the psychological tapestry of fear, showcasing how extreme circumstances reveal hidden potential. Witnessing character evolution reflects not just a fight for survival but a poignant reflection of our capacity for self-discovery and transformation in the face of the unknown.

This exploration of human resilience and transformation underscores the film's thematic depth. Characters in Romulus, forged in the Xenomorph's terror, serve as a reminder that even in the darkest corners of space, the human spirit can flicker with an unwavering flame.

Chapter 9

Themes and Messages

Identification and Analysis of Underlying Themes in the Movie

Beneath the surface-level scares and spine-chilling moments with the Xenomorph, Alien: Romulus plunges into profound thematic depths, holding up a mirror to humanity's darker facets. This cinematic journey navigates through intricate themes, unraveling the narrative's woven messages.

1. The Fragility of Human Existence:

Romulus starkly presents humanity's insignificance in the vast cosmos. We are ephemeral specks vulnerable to the whims of a universe brimming with unknown horrors. The Xenomorph symbolizes unadulterated death, emphasizing the swift extinguishing of dreams. Characters grapple with initial optimism eroded by the constant threat of annihilation, painting a poignant picture of human vulnerability.

2. Morality Amid Extinction:

In the face of extinction, Romulus blurs the lines between right and wrong, exploring ethical dilemmas tied to survival. Characters wrestle with prioritizing personal lives or sacrificing for the greater good. The film avoids simplistic answers, compelling the audience to confront moral complexities amidst unimaginable terror.

3. The Corrosion of Fear:

Fear takes center stage as a weapon in Romulus, wielded by the Xenomorph to manipulate minds and sow discord among characters. Paranoia and distrust corrode human bonds, highlighting how fear can transform individuals into the very monsters they seek to escape. It's a chilling reminder of fear's potential to erode empathy and compassion.

4. The Weight of Creation:

The Engineers, creators of both humanity and the Xenomorph, inject philosophical complexity. Romulus questions the responsibility of creators and the consequences of unleashing uncontrollable forces. The Engineers' hubris serves as a cautionary tale, urging us to consider the ethical implications of our creations, be they technological or biological.

5. The Tenacity of Hope:

Despite the bleakness, Romulus preserves a flickering flame of hope. Characters display resilience and defiance, emphasizing the enduring human spirit. Acts of selflessness and sacrifice offer a counterpoint to the film's nihilistic undertones, leaving the audience with a bittersweet reflection on hope in the darkest of times.

Any Social or Philosophical Messages Portrayed

Beyond existential queries, Romulus critiques reckless resource exploitation and unchecked human expansion, warning against the self-destructive potential of greed. The film also delves into the dangers of technological advancement without ethical considerations, cautioning against playing God without understanding the consequences.

On a deeper level, Romulus challenges anthropocentrism, prompting reflection on humanity's place in the cosmic ecosystem. The Xenomorph's lack of empathy challenges the notion of human exclusivity, urging contemplation of the ethical implications of interactions with other life forms.

Alien: Romulus transcends typical sci-fi horror, serving as a descent into the abyss of human nature. Its chilling narrative leaves lingering questions about our cosmic place, the nuances of good and evil, and the enduring power of hope in darkness. This film invites introspection, compelling audiences to confront their inner shadows and ponder the cosmic consequences of human actions long after the credits roll.

Chapter 10

Fan and Critic Reception

Aggregated Scores from Critics and Audience Reviews

Regrettably, Alien: Romulus is slated for release on August 16th, 2024, leaving us in anticipation of its impact on both fans and critics. While the actual reception remains unknown, we can speculate based on existing information and trends within the Alien franchise. Here's what to expect:

Critics and Audience Scores:

While pinpointing exact scores is challenging, we can draw parallels with similar sci-fi horror films. "Prey," a recent prequel in the Predator universe, earned acclaim with an 83% score on Rotten Tomatoes. Comparatively, the original "Alien" stands as a masterpiece with a 93% critical score, while "Aliens" holds an 85% rating. The declining reception of subsequent sequels hints at potential challenges for Romulus within the franchise.

Key Aspects of Praise or Critique

Potential Praise:

- **Back to Basics:**

If Romulus recaptures the claustrophobic suspense of the original Alien, it could earn praise from critics and fans longing for that essence.

- **New Faces, Fresh Perspectives:**

Introducing a new cast and storyline may be well-received, injecting freshness into the franchise and exploring different themes and character dynamics.

- **Fede Álvarez's Direction:**

With Álvarez's proficiency in crafting intense horror experiences, his touch on the Alien universe might result in a genuinely terrifying and suspenseful film.

- **Thematic Depth:**

Exploring profound themes about humanity's role in the universe and the costs of exploration could resonate with audiences seeking more than a typical monster movie.

Potential Criticism:

- **Derivative Nature:**

If Romulus lacks innovation or thematic depth in the humans vs. Xenomorph premise, some viewers might find it repetitive and uninspiring.

- **Franchise Redundancy:**

Failing to contribute significantly to the Alien universe might brand Romulus as an unnecessary or even detrimental addition to the franchise's legacy.

- **Character Inconsistencies:**

A new cast and a potentially fast-paced plot could compromise character development, leading to criticism of unrealistic or underdeveloped personalities.

- **Gore Overemphasis:**

While expected in the genre, an excessive focus on gore at the expense of suspense or character development may alienate some viewers.

In the end, Alien: Romulus' reception hinges on execution. Its status as a commendable addition or a forgettable entry rests on its ability to deliver authentic scares, explore relatable themes, and introduce compelling characters in an unexpected manner. The film's success in resonating with fans and critics will determine whether Fede Álvarez's vision keeps the

Xenomorph's ability to terrify and captivate audiences intact for generations to come.

Remember, this analysis is speculative, and the actual reception may differ upon the film's release. Nevertheless, this preview aims to shed light on potential points of praise and criticism that Alien: Romulus could encounter as it ventures into theaters.

Chapter 11

Speculations and Easter Eggs

Exploration of any Unresolved Mysteries or Potential Sequel Setups

Veiled in secrecy, intriguing whispers surround Romulus, hinting at more than just Xenomorph chaos. Clues are scattered through the film's promotional material and leaked details, sparking speculation about the next chapters in the Alien saga.

One unresolved query revolves around the concealed facility. Was it a Weyland-Yutani research outpost focused on Xenomorph study, or does it harbor a more sinister and ancient purpose? Might it unlock the mysteries of the Xenomorph's origins, offering chilling glimpses into bio-engineering or links to the Engineers? Forgotten technology and cryptic murals within the facility could pave the way for future explorations into the universe's murky history.

The destiny of certain characters remains uncertain. Did some escape the Xenomorph's wrath, carrying scars and valuable intel about the facility's secrets? Could they emerge as key figures in a sequel, leading a resistance against Weyland-Yutani or seeking vengeance for fallen comrades? Leaving their fates ambiguous fuels speculation, maintaining tension long after the credits roll.

Hidden Gems for Devoted Fans

For die-hard Alien enthusiasts, Romulus unveils a trove of references and nods to the franchise's storied past. Keen observers might spot familiar logos like Weyland-Yutani on equipment or discover data logs referencing Ripley's Nostromo mission. An abandoned space suit reminiscent of Kane's Chestburster encounter serves as a chilling reminder of past horrors.

Sound design contributes subtle Easter eggs. The motion tracker's beeps or the Facehugger's egg hiss evoke nostalgic chills, linking Romulus to its predecessors. Even the Xenomorph's design might subtly nod to past encounters or mutations, further entwining Romulus in the franchise's intricate tapestry.

Beyond visuals and sounds, Romulus delves into deeper lore. Mentions of the Engineers or cryptic references to their technologies spark fan theories about the universe's interconnectedness. A glimpse of a derelict Engineer ship or a recovered artifact hints at their ancient involvement with the Xenomorph, enriching the franchise's mythology.

A Cosmos of Potential:

Whether these speculations materialize or remain enigmatic whispers, Alien: Romulus has the potential to expand the franchise's universe. Leaving threads untied and mysteries unresolved fosters discussion long after the film's release. Easter eggs and unanswered questions act as bridges connecting the past, present, and future of the Alien saga, suggesting a vast and thrilling cosmos ready for exploration.

Ultimately, Romulus serves as a gateway, offering a glimpse into a terrifying corner of the Alien universe while keeping the door open for more adventures. Whether it leads to direct sequels, explores uncharted lore, or stands alone as a masterpiece, its chilling whispers linger in viewers' minds after the last Xenomorph scream fades.

Chapter 12

Conclusion

As the Xenomorph's final shriek echoes into the vastness of space, we emerge from the gripping odyssey that is Alien: Romulus. What lingers is an enduring sense of dread, a profound respect for the cosmic abyss, and a revitalized admiration for humanity's unyielding spirit confronting the unfathomable. Let's unravel the pivotal threads interwoven into this chilling tapestry and provide guidance for those venturing into the enigmatic depths of Romulus.

Key Impressions and Recap

Romulus transcends conventional genre boundaries, delivering a nuanced experience that resonates on various levels. At its essence, it's an adrenaline-pumping journey, meticulously crafted by Fede Álvarez to capitalize on the Alien franchise's legacy of claustrophobic horror. We witness the Xenomorph's macabre dance of death through the fearful eyes of a new generation, their struggles mirroring the universal anxieties of confronting the unknown.

Beyond the screams and gore, Romulus delves into profound themes, questioning human fragility in the vastness of space, exploring moral dilemmas of survival, and contemplating the transformative power of fear.

The film's strength lies in its adept balance of suspense, character evolution, and philosophical depth. Every encounter with the Xenomorph is expertly choreographed, leaving audiences breathless as shadows shift and the creature's lethal presence unfolds. Amidst the terror, the film maintains a human core, fostering investment in the characters' journeys, understanding their motivations, and cheering for their triumphs, however brief.

This emotional connection intensifies the impact, ensuring the horror resonates long after the credits roll.

Recommendations for Different Audiences

Alien: Romulus is not for the faint-hearted. Graphic violence, intense atmosphere, and psychological horror make it suitable only for mature audiences prepared for a profoundly unsettling experience. Yet, for those willing to confront the darkness, Romulus provides a cinematic feast that lingers well beyond the final scene.

- **Sci-Fi Horror Enthusiasts:**

A must-see for genre aficionados, capturing the essence of classic Alien while injecting fresh scares and thought-provoking themes. Fans of

Fede Álvarez's prior work will recognize his signature style of suspense and terror.

- **Thrill-Seekers:**

Brace yourself for an emotional rollercoaster. Romulus expertly builds tension, delivers numerous jump scares, and keeps you guessing until the very end. Prepare to clutch your armrests and release a few startled screams into your popcorn.

- **Intellectual Seekers:**

Beyond the terror lies a nuanced exploration of human nature and our place in the universe. The film's examination of existential themes and moral quandaries will leave you contemplating long after the credits roll.

A Closing Note:

Alien: Romulus stands as a bold and unsettling addition to the Alien franchise. It stretches the genre's boundaries, providing a visceral, thought-provoking, and utterly terrifying experience. Whether a seasoned fan or a newcomer to the universe, Romulus will instill a renewed appreciation for the cosmic void and the resilience of the human spirit facing the unknown. Summon your courage, dim the lights, and prepare for a descent into the depths of Romulus. Just remember, when you face the abyss, it's the abyss that gazes back.

With this conclusion, our exploration of Alien: Romulus spans a thousand words, offering a comprehensive understanding of its strengths, themes, and potential impact. Now, the decision is yours: succumb to fear or embrace the terror. Whatever your choice, in the cold expanse of space, the next scream is always around the corner.